You Have What It Takes!

A 21 Day Discovery of Your Greatest Self

Dr. Jamie T. Pleasant; Ph.D.

You Have What It Takes!

A 21 Day Discovery of Your Greatest Self

Dr. Jamie T. Pleasant; Ph.D.

You Have What It Takes! A 21 Day Discovery of Your Greatest Self

Copyright © 2017 by Dr. Jamie T. Pleasant; Ph.D.

Biblion Publishing LLC

All rights reserved. No portion of this book may be reproduced, stored in a retrieval system or transmitted in any form or by any means — electronic, mechanical, photocopy, recording or other without the prior written authorization of the author — except for a brief quotation in printed reviews.

Unless otherwise indicated, scripture quotations are from the Holy Bible, New International Version.

ISBN-978-194069810-6

Table of Contents

Day 1	You Were Born With A Vision	15
Day 2	There's Nothing You Can't Do	21
Day 3	All You Will Ever Need Is Already Inside of You	25
Day 4	You Are Full of Wonder	31
Day 5	You Were Created to Conquer	35
Day 6	You Were Born to Go Through Change	39
Day 7	You Are A Natural Born Problem Solver	45
Day 8	You Were Created to Do Great Things	51
Day 9	You Were Born to Lead	55
Day 10	Let Your Light Shine In Dark Places	59
Day 11	Shake Your Money Maker	65
Day 12	Don't Doubt, Do Trust	71
Day 13	Never Be In Want for Anything	77
Day 14	You Were Born To Be On Top	83

Table of Contents

Day 15	You Are Rooted In Purpose	87
Day 16	Stay Positive	93
Day 17	Get Your Expectations Up	97
Day 18	Don't Sell Yourself Short	101
Day 19	Be Thankful	105
Day 20	Know Where Your Help Comes From	109
Day 21	Image Is Everything	113

You Have What It Takes!

Do you have a vision to do something great? Do you dream of living a more prosperous and fulfilling life? Are you ready to experience peace, joy and happiness like you never have before? Do you feel in your heart that you are destined for more? If you are, this book is for you! *You Have What It Takes!: A 21 Day Discovery of Your Greatest Self* will take you on a 21 day discovery to release the greatest you that has been waiting to show itself for a very long time. You will grow as you meditate on words of wisdom that will inspire you to reach new heights! You will learn new ways to make decisions. You will walk in a newness of confidence and joy. You will walk into your destiny assured that you are accomplishing everything that you were ever born to do. You will realize that, *"You Have What it Takes!"*

Dedication

To my Daddy, Anthony T. Pleasant who was a perfect example to me of a real man. To my wife Kimberly, my two sons; Christian and Zion, and daughter, Nacara.

To the New Zion Christian Church Family, Clark Atlanta University and Lisa Nicole Cloud, a true friend!

Humbly Yours in Christ,

Apostle Jamie T. Pleasant

Getting the most out of
"You Have What It Takes!"

Congratulations on purchasing this book! Get ready to take your life to a new level. You can use this book for personal growth or group study sessions. Each day you will find a unique truth that will unlock your greatest self that has been waiting to be revealed for such a time as this in your life. This book includes 21 wisdom packed days of principles, meditations and exercises that will enhance your ability to live a new life beginning right now!

Day 1

You Were Born With A Vision

You were born to dream. You were born to have a vision about your future. Vision is what gives us a reason and hope to live! You were born to walk in a confident state after receiving your dreams until they become a reality for you over time. Since this is true, then, why do most of us have a problem telling others about the future things that will happen to us? The reason we have a problem telling others about the future that we know we will have, is because we have never understood how our future can speak to us right now! Yes! That is it! We don't know how to detect when our future is speaking to us. And, if we don't know when our future is speaking to us, we have no clue what our future holds. Being able to listen to our future speaking to us is relatively simple. We must simply not be afraid to dream. We must learn that one of the most precious times in our lives that we experience nightly, is when we lay our heads on our pillows and go to sleep. It is when we sleep that our physical capacity surrenders to the spiritual world. Yes! A dream is a spiritual event that is trying to make a way in our minds so that we can become impregnated in order to give birth to something natural.

> **A dream is a spiritual event that is trying to make a way in our minds so that we can become impregnated in order to give birth to something natural.**

Once a dream can penetrate our subconscious and reach our mind, we will be in the process of taking that which is spiritual and converting it into a physical reality. We will actually convert that dream into a manifested reality of our life. Therefore, cherish all of your dreams and never take any of them for granted. As you are dreaming and after your dream, try to engage your mind about what is taking place or has taken place. Next, journal your dreams on paper and watch and wait as they come to pass. One of the biggest secrets in the universe is that most of our dreams never come to reality because we fail to journal or write them down. Don't stop dreaming, but start writing after you dream. Write until you feel your future! Write until

You Were Born With A Vision

you get your blessing! Write until you see your future! Though it may take some time, it will not take long for your future to become your today. We must never forget that our future will never get ahead of us. Our future will never leave us behind. It has been ordained to always, always, always, be right on time. Our future is simply waiting for us to WRITE it down on paper and wait for it to come to pass. Below, write about a dream you had recently. Write your entire dream down very plainly. Write things that you were not clear about in the dream. Ask God to reveal the meaning of your dreams to you clearly and plainly. Remember, a vision can't become a reality until you have the courage and the energy to give it life through passion, planning and execution.

Habakkuk 2:3 (KJV)
For the vision is yet for an appointed time, but at the end it shall speak, and not lie: though it tarry, wait for it; because it will surely come, it will not tarry.

Write below your thoughts on what you discovered about your *"greatest self"* today.

_____

You Were Born With A Vision

You Were Born With A Vision

Day 2

There's Nothing That You Can't Do

Have you ever found yourself tired and not able to get up enough energy to do something? Have you ever been at the point of giving up concerning a matter that you just couldn't seem to find a resolution to? If so, then you must tap into the reality that you have been created to be able to do anything. We must never confuse tiredness with inadequacy. We must never become frustrated when it seems like we don't have the strength to face some things in our lives.

> **We must never confuse tiredness with inadequacy**

Believe it or not; it is when we get to the point that our energy and strength are zapped, or we are completely empty and have lost our zeal for something; we have just set ourselves up to be able to deal with whatever we are struggling with. That's right! When it seems like we have lost all of our strength, we are in the perfect position to tap into overdrive and find an unlimited amount of power and strength in Christ. Christ is the difference maker between us being reenergized or falling flat on our face. The word Christ is not Jesus' last name or just a simple title. The word Christ means; empowered to perform for God. Yes! We will become empowered with supernatural strength to perform anything when we are at our wits end.

> **The word Christ means empowered to perform for God.**

It is when we are at this point of emptiness and tiredness; we must simply call on Jesus and ask that His Christ power will be poured out on us through the Holy Spirit. Again, all we have to do is find enough strength to call on Christ and the power of the Christ be poured into us, and we can then perform. It is just that simple. You see, the secret to us having the ability to tap into a reservoir of unlimited power is simply having enough energy and humility to call on the Christ so that His power can be released on us to perform. Therefore, when you are tired; don't give up, call on Christ. When you are frustrated; don't get mad, call on

There's Nothing That You Can't Do

Christ. When you are faced with difficult decisions; don't rush and decide wrongly out of confusion, call on Christ. Call on Christ and renew your strength. Practice below what you will say to tap into the power of Christ when you are tired and need renewed energy and strength.

Philippians 4:13 (KJV)
I can do all things through Christ who strengthens me.

Write below your thoughts on what you discovered about your *"greatest self"* today.

_____

_____

_____

_____

_____

_____

_____

There's Nothing That You Can't Do

Day 3

All You Will Ever Need Is Already Inside of You

There are times when we are in need of things to help make our lives complete. We need food, water, shelter, love, clothes and other things. We usually become aware that we need something when we experience a tugging in our heart for it. You may feel a tugging or desire in your heart for a new car, new job, house, career, clothes, more peace, joy, etc. However, you may question yourself as to how you will be able to get these things you need or desire. You may even look at your abilities and resources and plainly see that you don't have what it takes to get to the next level of your life. Here is where you must realize the secret that exists in a need you may have. First, when a need becomes apparent in our lives, it is God that has placed that need in our heart.

> **When a need becomes apparent in our lives, it is God that has placed that need in our heart in order for us to go to a new level in life.**

He created that need in us because it is time for Him to take us to the next level. That need, then takes the form of a want or desire that we can't shake or get rid of. We then find ourselves in a very uncomfortable state. We become anxious, uncomfortable and sometimes even irritable. These things will occur because God is making sure that we won't miss the blessing that He has for us. We can either let these tensions get the best of us, or we can extinguish them by pursuing a higher level in life. The secret to going to new levels in our lives has already been placed inside of us. We must now tap into the glory of God and pull out the riches that have been placed in us. Now get this! It is at this point that we must come to God and make contact with His glory. What is His glory? It is the nature and essence of who He is. God's glory is His presence that we will experience as we come into contact with His goodness, mercy, compassion and love. Therefore, we must come to him and isolate ourselves in a quiet place. We should next

All You Will Ever Need Is Already Inside of You

focus on Him and wait until we feel His presence. As we begin to feel His presence, we will feel His love, goodness, mercy and compassion. At this point, we should praise Him, call on Him, thank Him and then confidently let Him know that we depend on Him and expect Him to supply our needs through His glory. Next, we should take advantage of the riches that exist for us to behold when we have tapped into His glory. It is at this point we should make contact with His glory and release all of the stored up things that we will need to go to the next level of our lives. This is how we can tap into His glorious riches and get blessed. The riches of His glory will release our joy, peace, love, house, car, good health, clothes and other things that we need, want and desire. You should not be afraid to tap into the glory of God and pull out the riches of His glory to live a better life right now. Remember, His glory, which contains riches to meet our needs, wants and desires have been placed on the inside of us. All that we will ever need is within us. His glorious riches are waiting for us to tap into the presence of God that is incased in our being. Tap into God's glory and pull out your blessings! Below write what needs you are experiencing right now. Then, let God

All You Will Ever Need Is Already Inside of You

know that you are ready for those needs to be supplied through His glorious riches. Begin the process of receiving your blessings and write down what you experience.

Philippians 4:19 (KJV)
But my God shall supply all your need according to his riches in glory by Christ Jesus.

Write below your thoughts on what you discovered about your *"greatest self"* today.

_____

_____

_____

_____

_____

_____

_____

_____

All You Will Ever Need Is Already Inside of You

All You Will Ever Need Is Already Inside of You

Day 4

You Are Full of Wonder

Take a moment and realize that you are not a half put together person. You are not made half-heartedly. You are not an afterthought of God. You are fearfully and wonderfully made.

> **You are not an afterthought of God. You have been made out of wonder and you are full of wonder.**

You have been made out of wonder and you are full of wonder. The Biblical meaning of the word wonder is firm, hard, and marvelous. Therefore, we should be firm and hard when facing difficult circumstances. Out of our firmness, people should marvel at how we have overcome the obstacles that we have faced. We show marvel by responding positively to something that has negatively tried to disrupt our lives. We show marvel by producing a supernatural response to a natural phenomenon. Now, knowing this, we must learn how to respond based on who

You Are Full of Wonder

we are and what has been placed in us. We are wonderfully made and made out of wonder. Therefore, that which anyone is made of should be a natural overflow in his/her life. Have you ever wondered why you face so many trying circumstances in your life? Have you ever wondered why it seems like your back is always up against a wall? It is because God has ordained such events to take place so you can see what you are made of. You can't produce a WONDER in your life if you aren't faced with a challenge or event that looks hopeless. It is in these times that you have to call from within yourself and produce the wonder that you are made out of. So, the next time you are facing a challenging or hopeless situation, show your true self and produce some WONDER.

Write below how you have responded to unforeseen events that challenged you in the past. Now, knowing that you are full of wonder, write down below how you will respond to any unforeseen events that may be a challenge to you in the future.

You Are Full of Wonder

Psalms 139:14
I praise you because I am fearfully and <u>wonderfully</u> made; your works are <u>wonderful,</u> I know that full well.

You Are Full of Wonder

Day 5

You Were Created To Conquer

What does it mean to be a conqueror? It means to overcome. That means, whatever life may throw at us regardless of how hard it may seem; we will get over it. To get over it means that we may have been hurt by something; we may have been turned down by someone or even challenged by some unforeseen circumstance. However, at the end of the battle that we have faced, we will be victors over it and become much stronger. We will have the victory over it and get over the ill effects of having been in a battle. That is the beauty of conquering something. Being a conqueror doesn't mean we won't face the same challenges again; it means that we won't feel the pain, hurt and ill effects of the battle ever again because it will have very minor negative effects in our lives. However, to stop here is to miss who we truly are. We are not just conquerors! Not at all. We are more than conquerors. What does that mean? The meaning of more than a conqueror comes from the Greek word, *hypernikaō*. This means to gain a surpassing victory over our enemy, foe or obstacle. Therefore, we must take on a new attitude that we are not born or made to face the same obstacles repeatedly.

> **We are not born or made to face the same obstacles repeatedly.**

If we face the same obstacles repeatedly, that would mean that we are not progressing in our lives. It would mean that we have become static in our growth, achievements and pursuits. No! As conquerors, we have gained a surpassing victory over all of our challenges in that we have moved on to bigger and better things in our lives. Little things that we dealt with months ago, can't affect us anymore because we are no longer in a position to be affected by them. We have surpassed them. Things we dealt with last year can't hurt us this year. Things that bothered us last year should bring joy to us now. Things that used to make us lose sleep, now doesn't affect our sleep anymore. Yes! We are more than conquerors through Christ Jesus! We have gained a surpassing victory over things that we dealt with in our

You Were Created To Conquer

past. We are so far ahead of them that they can only look at us from a distance. All these negative things must now watch us celebrate our new territories of accomplishments as well. Negative things must sit back and look at us as we triumphantly overcome new challenges and conquer new obstacles every day. Yes! We were born to be more than conquerors! Write down below on how you will overcome any obstacle you might face based on your new, *"more than a conqueror's"* spirit.

Romans 8:36-37

As it is written: "For your sake we face death all day long; we are considered as sheep to be slaughtered." 37 No, in all these things we are more than conquerors through him who loved us.

_____

_____

_____

_____

_____

You Were Created To Conquer

Day 6

You Were Born To Go Through Change

The pressures of life can suck the life right out of you. There are so many things we have to deal with in our daily lives. We have to deal with pressures on the job, financial obligations, taking care of the children, maintaining a good marriage, helping others, and many other things. As a result, we often feel as though the very life that is supposed to give us vitality is being sucked right out of us. Here is where we need to understand the purpose of the pressures that we may experience sometimes. Pressure is defined as a force that one can feel that changes the state of one thing to another state. For example, any meteorologist will tell you that they are able to predict the weather based on barometric pressure changes that they measure. Also, it is pressure that causes a solid to change to a liquid or gas in chemistry. That is why water can be changed into ice as well as steam. It is based simply on the effects of pressure.

You Were Born To Go Through Change

If we were to take a tire and not put any air in it and roll a two-ton car over it, the tire would be destroyed and would crack into pieces. However, if we were to put air in that same tire, something different would occur. It is the air pressure that we put in a tire that allows our car to be driven down a road. It is amazing but a tire with only 38 pounds per square inch of air in it can support a two-ton vehicle. One would think that the two-ton vehicle would cause the tire to burst. However, it doesn't because the air placed in the tire changes the nature of the tire to be able to handle the pressure being applied to it. Therefore, we must realize that as we face the pressures of life and feel hard pressed, we are not supposed to crack under pressure but rise to the occasion just like a tire on a car. We experience pressure in our lives in order for change to occur in our lives. Therefore, the next time you feel a lot of pressure; don't let it get you down.

> **We experience pressure in our lives in order for change to occur in our lives.**

Get excited and get ready, because you are about to rise to a new level in your life. Get ready to rise to a new financial

You Were Born To Go Through Change

position! Get ready to rise to a new level of joy! Get ready to rise to a new level of peace! Get ready and remember that you carry the ability to automatically inflate yourself to a new level of success within your own body. Never forget that the ability to tap into your new life is not on the outside of you but on the inside of you as **2 Corinthians 4: 10 says,**

We always carry around in our body the death of Jesus, so that the life of Jesus may also be revealed in our body.

Therefore, never forget the purpose of pressure in your life. When you feel it, get ready to rise to a new level of success. Reach down inside yourself and inflate your mind, soul and spirit so that you can carry the new load of success in your life as you travel down life's highway of blessings!

Below, write down the pressures that you have been experiencing and list a plan of action to deal with each one as you rise to a new level in your life. Write down how you will pull from within yourself the ability to rise to a new level of life.

2 Corinthians 4:8-10

We are hard pressed on every side, but not crushed; perplexed, but not in despair; [9] persecuted, but not abandoned; struck down, but not destroyed. [10] We always carry around in our body the death of Jesus, so that the life of Jesus may also be revealed in our body.

You Were Born To Go Through Change

Day 7

You Are A Natural Born Problem Solver

How often do you find yourself confused, puzzled or overwhelmed with something? Have you ever felt so overwhelmed with something you had to do, that it just ate away at you? If so, you need to remind yourself that you are a natural born problem solver. Yes! We have been designed by God to solve problems. When the human mind has to solve a problem, it is stimulated and energized with electronic impulses that rush through our entire mental system. It is this type of stimulation that causes growth in us mentally. In other words, the more problems that we have to solve, the more stimulation and mental growth we will experience. It is a proven fact that the more we engage our minds, the longer we live and are able to develop a higher mental capacity. Studies have shown that people that engage in problem solving skills are less prone to mental diseases as well. We are natural born problem solvers and when we are engaging our minds in certain areas, we will achieve the highest level of certain things that God has planned for us. Even Adam while in the Garden of Eden was faced with a problem at the beginning of his existence. He had to figure out what to call each animal that had been created. Imagine how overwhelming it had to be for Adam to do that. He had to name every animal a different and unique name. However, he didn't have any problem naming any of the animals. He easily named them because he tapped on the inside of himself and realized that he was a natural born problem solver. In fact, he knew that naming the animals wouldn't cause him to experience any anxiety or despair. To be in a state of despair means that he would be facing a problem with no hope of ever finding a solution. In fact, he would have been easily facing failure if he had taken a negative attitude about naming the animals. It is very interesting to note that Adam had to prove to God that he could handle the problem of naming all the animals before he could go on to a bigger challenge. We must never forget that problems and challenges that we experience, are training tools that God uses to grow us and prepare us for bigger blessings! God was training him for a bigger challenge that was coming very soon.

> **Problems and challenges that we experience are God's training tools that He uses to grow us and prepare us to be able to handle bigger blessings!**

It was only after Adam rose to the challenge of naming all the animals on earth that God allowed him to name his wife. How beautiful that must have been. But note that he could only name his wife after proving he could handle the task of naming the animals. Adam named his wife woman and then Eve. Woman, which means, out of the womb of man, was the perfect name for her. Why? Because it was a reminder of who she was and who he was. It meant that both of them would always know that they needed each other and could never be whole without each other. Thank God he didn't name her Whale or Donkey. That would have been a mess. Why? Biblical evidence shows us that a person's name is a description of who they are and what they will become. Now, what current problems are you facing that seem overwhelming to you? Is it an exam in school, marriage decision, financial decision, job choice or home buying decision? If so, don't be overwhelmed. Be encouraged! Tap deep down inside of yourself and find the hope, promise and assurance that God has worked out an answer for all the challenges you may face. Tap inside of yourself and find the life of Christ that says that you will find hope in any situation that you may be facing. All we have to do is give our concerns to the Lord and let Him instruct us. As a result, solutions and peace will begin to flow from within us, and we will rise to every occasion that rears its head up against us and our peace. Remember, problems are God's way of preparing us for a promotion in life so that we can live better. We must always wait and hear the solution from God before we move forward. Below, write some problems that you are facing and describe how you will not let anxiety or despair ruin your blessing from God.

2 Corinthians 4:8-10

We are perplexed, but not in despair;
[9] persecuted, but not abandoned; struck down, but not destroyed. [10] We always carry around in our body the death of Jesus, so that the life of Jesus may also be revealed in our body.

You Are A Natural Born Problem Solver

You Are A Natural Born Problem Solver

Day 8

You Were Created To Do Great Things

We were created to do great things in this lifetime. We were not created to be mediocre. We were not created to be average. We were not created to just get by or make it. We were created to do great things; things that are great and noteworthy! Yes! You were created to do things that others would appreciate and admire. If this is the case, then why do so many people go through their lifetime only achieving average things? Why do so many people live and then die without leaving a legacy of their uniqueness on this earth? The answers to these questions lie in the fact that most people fail to realize that God created them to do great works. He created us to do great things! God gave us the ability to do things easily that others would find very difficult to do. That is the blessing that exists inside of us. We hold inside of us the ability to do certain things better than others. This is our uniqueness that sets us apart. This is where our blessings lie. Each one of us has been created by God to do something more skillfully than another person. As a result, every one of us will be able to help others because we specialize in doing something easily and with excellence that others have a hard time doing. Therefore, we should strive to tap into the greatness that God has placed in us. Do you want to know where your greatness has been placed? Well, it was placed in you before you were born. God prepared in advance the ability for you to do great things before He formed you in your mother's womb. Now as we walk in time and begin to do certain things; all we have to do is watch and see if what we do flows and seems very easy to us. In other words, does it feel natural or come naturally to you? If it does, you have found your great and unique work. If you can effortlessly do something well that others have a hard time doing, you have found your greatness.

> **If you can effortlessly do something well that others have a hard time doing, you have found your greatness.**

You Were Created To Do Good Things

If they try to do what we do, and it causes undue stress to them, then we have found our greatness. If we experience a sense of completeness and joy when we do something, we have found our greatness. Get out there and do your great thing! Do your great work! Make your mark in life that others will admire and remember you for! Below, write some things that you do and know that you are great at. Are the great things that you are currently doing providing an income for you? If not, you may be missing your true calling and financial blessing in life. Write below your thoughts on what you discovered about your *"greatest self"* today.

Ephesians 2:10
For we are God's workmanship, created in Christ Jesus to do good works, which God prepared in advance for us to do.

_____

_____

_____

You Were Created To Do Good Things

Day 9

You Were Born To Lead

We are natural born leaders. We have been created to head many things. We are never truly being who God designed us to be until we start taking a leadership role in something. Not only are we created to lead things, we are called to perform them with excellence. We are not only created to head things but to excel in that which we head. Therefore, you must begin to tap into your God given leadership abilities and fully express your uniqueness to a watching world. You may ask yourself, "What should I be leading?" Well, you can start out by leading yourself. Begin to lead yourself by expecting better things in your life. Lead yourself by taking risks that will give you a better lifestyle.

> **Lead yourself by taking risks that will give you a better lifestyle.**

Lead yourself by taking new classes to prepare for a better future. After leading yourself; lead your family. If you are a wife and mother, lead your children. Lead them by training and teaching them by example as you operate in excellence. If you are a father, lead your wife and children by spiritually teaching and presenting the thoughts, teachings, and ways of God to them. Once we have led ourselves, we can become leaders in our communities and jobs. We should never forget that leading others should be by example, not just a title. We are all called and expected to operate as a leader somewhere in our lives. Therefore, tap into the leadership ability that God has already placed in you and make a difference in your life and everybody else's life that comes into contact with you. Write down below the areas that you currently serve as a leader. Write down areas in your life where you need to take more of a leadership role. Finally, write below how you can tap into the leadership ability that has already been placed on the inside of you.

Deuteronomy 28:13

The Lord will make you the head, not the tail. If you pay attention to the commands of the Lord your God that I give you this day and carefully follow them, you will always be at the top, never at the bottom.

You Were Born To Lead

Day 10

Let Your Light Shine In Dark Places

Do you know that you are the light of the world? Yes, you are! Just what does that mean? It means that we are expected to give light or illuminate all things we come into contact with. To give light means that we are to bring things out which others can't see. We are called to be problem solvers, joy igniters and path finders. You were designed to be the one that others can come to and get solutions to their problems. You are the one that others should look to when things seem hopeless. You are the one that others should seek out when they are trying to choose a course of action or make a decision. How is your light? Is it shining or hidden underneath your own problems, struggles, disappointments and challenges? We must make sure that we never let personal challenges snuff out our light. Our light should be able to outshine any trouble or challenge that we face.

Let Your Light Shine In Dark Places

> **Our light should be able to outshine any trouble or challenge that we face.**

We must first look at light as anything that is positive, good and joyful. We can also define darkness as anything that is evil, hurtful and damaging. Having defined the two that way, let's look at how we can begin to exercise the light that is on the inside of us. We must never forget that a doubting world is looking at us to see if we can take a dark situation and turn it into light. They are also looking at us to see if we will surrender to darkness and be defeated by it. When faced with troubles, problems and challenges, most people are overcome by darkness versus tapping into the power of the internal light that is on the inside of them. Most people think in their minds that darkness is more powerful than light. This is simply not true. For example, if you were to enter into a dark room at night, you would not be able to see anything. Darkness literally has filled the room. If you are not careful, you will stumble and fall. It is amazing, but if the room is dark enough; even if your eyes are wide open, you will not be able to see anything. However, if you have a very small flashlight in your hand

Let Your Light Shine In Dark Places

and turn it on, all of a sudden you will see a ray of light that will create a path in the entire room that will not only penetrate the darkness in the room, but separate the darkness in the room as well. Now, please see the power in this. Light is so powerful that it literally can show itself in a room full of darkness and then separate the darkness. Do you see the power in this? We have the ability within ourselves to be in the middle of problems, struggles and challenges and reach down within ourselves and turn on the light. Once we turn on the light which can be in the form of joy or the ability to solve a problem, we will overcome the darkness and separate ourselves from the negative effect of whatever we are dealing with. We will then be able to walk progressively towards another level of life as darkness and its evilness will depart from out of our lives at that level. Therefore, the next time you are facing a problem, turn on your light. The next time you are hurt, turn on your light. The next time you face a challenge that has you weighed down, turn on your light. Make a doubting world a believer that there is something that is on the inside of you that says you will not surrender to a challenge. Let the world know that you have Christ's

Let Your Light Shine In Dark Places

power on the inside of you that allows you to cast a light so bright and strong that no darkness can withstand its presence. Let your light shine! Please write below some challenging situations you may be facing and list a plan of action to let your light shine the next time; instead of being overcome by the ill effects of the darkness.

Matthew 5:14
"You are the light of the world. A city on a hill cannot be hidden.

_____

_____

_____

_____

_____

_____

_____

Let Your Light Shine In Dark Places

Day 11

Shake Your Money Maker

We are called to be the salt of the earth. Salt is used for a variety of reasons. It is used most commonly to flavor food. Salt is also used to preserve certain meats and even provide a safer traveling surface on highways that are covered with ice. Salt is one of the few things that can change the state of something without losing its identity and effectiveness. If you were to take salt and put it on a table, it would simply sit right on top of the table and do nothing. It would just be plain salt on a table. However, if you take the salt and place it on meat, it will dissolve inside the meat and change the flavor of the meat without losing its effectiveness. How can salt not dissolve on the table but go inside meat and change the flavor even though it can't be seen anymore? This happens because salt has been designed to change its state from a solid to a liquid when it comes into contact with the right thing. Salt can bring out the best in other things without losing its identity of its true design. Salt also has preserving power when placed on meat to keep it from spoiling. We, like salt, are designed to be able to change the state of our thinking, spirit and disposition when we come into contact with certain things. We have been designed by God to be able to remain the same or retain our uniqueness when we come into contact with certain things while positively adding and changing the nature or state of those things we come into contact with. We have been designed to be able to judge whether we should get involved with certain people or things that we may come into contact with instantaneously.

> **We have been designed by God to be able to remain the same or retain our uniqueness when we come into contact with certain things while positively adding and changing the nature or state of those things we come into contact with.**

Let's look at the table example again. Just like the salt that comes into contact with the table, and it can't penetrate inside of it, we should know immediately if we are accepted by people or something we want to become a part of. Not only should we be accepted by them as a result of them letting us in like the salt going inside the meat, we should not lose our identity once we become a part of them as well. Start watching the people you come into contact with. Are they a hard table or good meat in your life? That is, are they hard, non-permeable and not open to receive your uniqueness, or are they meat? Are they open and eager to let you add value to their lives? Are they open to adding value to your life? If they are meat, you will be invited to become a part of them, and you will bring to the party a flavoring that will add to the group or thing that you are now a part of. They in turn will make you better as well. In other words, you will blend right in with them and add to the group without losing your uniqueness. You will bring flavor to the group and all of you will be better off than before you ever got together. Now don't miss this! You will become a part of them but not lose your identity and the effectiveness of your unique abilities. Be careful and watch who you hang out with and become a part of. They could either draw you in and rob you of your power or allow your uniqueness to add value to the group as you all evolve into a total divine expression of who you were created to be. Find your meat. That is, find the people that you are supposed to be in constant friendship with. Your salt is your gifts, talents and uniqueness. Your gifts, talents and uniqueness are your money makers. Let them come forward and you will prosper.

> **Your salt is your gifts, talents and uniqueness. Your gifts, talents and uniqueness are your money makers.**

Therefore, don't be afraid to let the real you come forward. Don't be afraid to shake your salt. When given a chance to make a difference, shake your money maker. When given a chance to show your skills, don't hold back. Shake your money maker. When given a chance to shine and be known as the expert, shake your money maker. Shake your talents! Shake your gifts! Shake your uniqueness! If you don't fully express yourself, you will be trampled on by everyone. You will never make the mark in the world you were destined to make. Finally, find a group of people where you will become all you were designed to be without losing any part of who you are.

> **Find a group of people where you will become all you were designed to be without losing any part of who you are.**

List below any groups that you belong to or friends that you associate with, that accept you for who you are. Write about how all of you are better off because of that. Next, make a list of the group of people, friends or even the job that you currently work at. List if you are accepted, not accepted, appreciated or struggling with belonging within that group, etc. Finally, list a plan of action to remove yourself from the group that you are not comfortable belonging to.

Matthew 5:13
"You are the salt of the earth. But if the salt loses its saltiness, how can it be made salty again? It is no longer good for anything, except to be thrown out and trampled by men.

_____

_____

Shake Your Money Maker

Day 12

Don't Doubt, Do Trust

How often are you faced with embarking on a new career, relationship, or pursuit? It is at these times that you must remember that you were designed to have faith and come into contact with the faith that has been placed in you. However, when faced with various new ventures in our lives, we easily fall into doubt. Doubt is defined as; to waver in the mind away from the original state of your mind.

> **Doubt is defined as; to waver in the mind away from the original state of your mind.**

Most of us don't have a problem with believing what God has told us to do. We don't even have a problem starting to do what He told us to do. It is when we begin to do what He has already told us to do, that problems begin to surface; as our thoughts become negative. In other words, our mind begins to battle with our spirit as to whether that which we are doing; will have a positive ending. We may even begin to wonder if what we are doing will fail. This mental battle always occurs after God has told us what to do. We must begin to tap into the faith that has been placed in us by God. We must stop letting doubt creep into our minds. Have you ever been excited about something and told someone about it just to have them remind you of the numerous things that could go wrong? Isn't it interesting how all of a sudden you begin to lose the excitement and confidence that you initially had? The problem is that we will tend to lean on the side of doubt versus stand on the faith of truth. A lot of times, we lean on doubt so much that we decide to quit that which God has called us to do. However, we must decide not to take the easy way out and quit when something seems like it is taking forever to be completed. The easy way out is to lean on what we know, touch or can see. However, it is much more difficult to tap into the power of faith by believing in something while confidently waiting for it to happen. It becomes more difficult to walk in faith when our surroundings are consistently showing us things that are contradictory to what we believe will happen.

Don't Doubt, Do Trust

Doubt is something that we can easily lean on. It is easy to lean on past hurts, rejections and disappointments. It is harder to stand on what we have never physically experienced before. It is hard to stand on the fact that the address we were born at, is not the address we were destined to live at. It is hard to stand on the fact that we will have more money in the bank in 5 years from now versus what we have in the bank right now. It may be hard to stand on the fact that you will complete a college degree when no one in your family has ever even gone to college. See! It is harder to stand on the truth than to lean on a doubt.

> **It is harder to stand on the truth than to lean on a doubt.**

Therefore, we must practice the truth that God has revealed to us through a dream, word or vision that we may have. If you dreamed about it, it will happen. If you had a vision about it, it is yours. If you received a word from God about it, it is yours. Now, whenever anyone comes to you and gives you a list of things that can go wrong; ignore them. They may even try and tell you that you can't do something.

You should look them in the eye and say, "You of little faith." "Can't you see that I have been given assurance by God that this thing I am pursuing is already mine?" "Can't you see that there is something on the inside of me that says I will not fail?" "Can't you see that my mind is made up about this and nothing can stop me; not even you?" Start operating with a new response to people and all the negative things they may say to you. Whenever, they say negative things to you; or tell you that you can't do something, reply to them this way, "Tell me I can't, and I'll show you I can." That's right! Hit them with the faith that says; you can do all things through Christ, whom gives you strength. Let them know that you can do something when they say that you can't. When you take this stand, watch and see if heaven will not open up right in front of your eyes and deliver your dream to you. All you have to do, is stand up and tell people what you believe in. Stand up and tell them it shall be done. Stand up and tell them that God will bring it to pass through you. Stand up and watch your blessings come down. Write down below how you will handle negative things that might try and infiltrate your mind concerning the promises of God in your life.

Don't Doubt, Do Trust

Matthew 14:31

Immediately Jesus reached out his hand and caught him. "You of little faith," he said, "why did you doubt?"

Don't Doubt, Do Trust

Day 13

Never Be In Want For Anything

We have been designed to never be in a state of continuously wanting the same thing without ever receiving it. First, we must recognize the three states of human life. There is a need state, a want state and a desire state. Here we will focus on the need and want states. The need level exists where we must have certain things in order to stay alive. For example, we need water, food, shelter, clothes, etc. Without these things, we would die. The next level or state of life is at the want stage. The want stage says that our needs have already been met at all levels. A want then is something that we pursue above the need level to achieve a higher level of satisfaction. For example, we need water to live, but we may want a soft drink for enjoyment and satisfaction. While water is good and healthy for us, we may want a soft drink because it adds spice to our lives. God Himself operates above the need level and designed us to do so as well. Before you say that you are content and happy living at the need level, let's take a moment to make sure you understand the significance in obtaining certain wants. For example, to get from one place to another, we can easily walk to a destination. However, we are limited by how far we can go if it is based on walking only. We need feet in order to walk. However, our feet will limit the amount of distance we can travel in a certain period of time. Therefore, most of us will want to have a car. But, all we needed was our two feet. So, we will most likely choose to operate at the want level. Not only can a car carry us from point A to point B, but when we arrive where we are going, we will have energy to enjoy ourselves when we arrive at our destination. We will have gotten there faster and the trip may even be more enjoyable because we chose to ride in a car versus walking. To go someplace further, faster and less laborious, we will want a car and get one. It is the same way in life. It is not just where you want to go in your life, but how you want to travel to get there.

Never Be In Want For Anything

> **It is not just where you want to go in your life, but how you want to travel to get there.**

You will want to be energized, refreshed and still youthful when you get to a certain place in your life. Therefore, you want certain things to make your life more enjoyable and satisfying. If you have dirty clothes, you need to wash them. You can scrub them on your hands with a wash board or thank God, you can put them in a washing machine. You need to wash them, but you want to enjoy the excitement of watching them become clean in a washing machine as you do other things. Therefore, never forget that God has created us to be able to live a satisfying and enjoyable life. We should want things that will make our lives easier, allow us to be more productive and bring us more satisfaction. Never feel guilty when you want to have something that will make your life more satisfying! Never feel guilty when you want a new car! Never feel guilty when you want a new home! Never feel guilty when you want a new coat! Go and get those things and know that you were designed to want certain things to show everyone that God the Father is a shepherd that cares for you and your wants. He wants you to live a satisfying and fulfilled life. Write below some things that you know God has placed on your heart to want. List them and rest in His ability to move through you to not only get those things, but keep them and enjoy them after you get them.

Psalms 23:1 (KJV)
The LORD *is* my shepherd; I shall not want.

_____

_____

_____

_____

_____

_____

_____

_____

Never Be In Want For Anything

Day 14

You Were Born To Be On Top

Do you ever wonder why you always want to win? Do you always seem to want more in your life? Why is it that you always get excited when you receive a promotion on your job? Well, the answer to all of these questions is very simple. You were created by God to be on TOP. Yes! We were created to be winners. We were created to be leaders. We were created to be successful. That is why we are always striving to do better and achieve bigger things. It is very interesting, but you have probably questioned yourself about why you always want more out of life. If you have, don't make the mistake and do what most people do. They fall into guilt, thinking that maybe they are being greedy or discontent with what they currently have. The truth is that, we will experience a desire to have more things and get promotions on our jobs because God designed us that way. In fact, when we feel the urge to go after something; it is

God's way of letting us know He has a blessing waiting for us.

> **When we feel the urge to go after something; it is God's way of letting us know He has a blessing waiting for us.**

All we have to do now is tap into the success that has been placed on the inside of us. In order to tap into the success that has been placed inside of us, we must simply believe we have all that it takes to rise to the challenge in order to have more. We will have to get our mind, soul, body and spirit ready to possess the new things that God wants us to have. We must ready our hearts. We must ready our hands. We must ready our eyes. We must ready these things to be able to enjoy, touch and see the new realities that God wants us to experience and possess. Therefore, never feel guilty when you have a desire to achieve. Never feel guilty when you get blessed. Never feel guilty when you get a promotion. God released all of those things in your life for you to enjoy yourself and help others. And remember, when you do your best and keep reaching for new heights, God will place you at the top and keep you at the top. In fact, when he places you at the top you will never see the bottom again. It has been often said that it is lonely at the top. However, you will quickly find out that it is not as lonely at the top as you may think it is. In fact, you will find a lot of people right there with you. Also, you will learn that it's a lot more fun up at the top as well. Go ahead, strive to get to the top, stay there and give God the glory for your ability to achieve! Below, list areas in your life that you feel that God is calling you to be placed at the top.

Deuteronomy 28:13
The Lord will make you the head, not the tail. If you pay attention to the commands of the Lord your God that I give you this day and carefully follow them, <u>you will always be at the top, never at the bottom.</u>

_____

_____

_____

_____

You Were Born To Be On Top

Day 15

You Are Rooted In Purpose

We have been birthed to know what our unique purpose in life is. Knowing and operating in our purpose is what gives us the ability to overcome any obstacle we may ever face. When we can tap into God's purpose for our lives, it will change our perspective on everything we may encounter. For example, there may be many things that you have experienced that were not pleasant at all. You may have lost a loved one in your life. You may have lost a job. You even may have gone through an illness that literally almost sucked the life right out of you. What was your reaction to these trying situations? How did you get through those tough times? Well, there is one thing for sure that you must never forget, if you want to go through certain rough times in your life and come out of them better off than before you experienced them. You must know and operate in God's unique purpose for your life.

You Are Rooted In Purpose

> **You must know and operate in God's unique purpose for your life.**

If you don't know what God's unique purpose for your life is, then just ask Him right now to reveal it to you. Take a moment and ask Him to show you what it is that He has purposed for you to do in this lifetime for Him? Please think more than inside a church building, ministry and the like. Think about practical everyday things that He may want you to accomplish. He may want you to be a great Dad. He may want you to own a business. He may even want you to stay on your job and become the boss. Open yourself up to whatever He says to you. When you accept His words of purpose for your life, you will see a change in the way you handle things. For example, things that used to get you down won't anymore, when you are in purpose! Things that used to suck the energy and life out of you; won't anymore, when you are in purpose! It doesn't matter what thing you may experience. It simply won't have power to negatively affect you anymore. Because in all things God will work it out for you to experience a good ending. So, what are you waiting for? Ask God to reveal

You Are Rooted In Purpose

to you His purpose for your life. Ask Him to tug at your heart to lead you in the right direction. Go ahead and get ready to experience a powerful and purposeful life! Below, write down how you want to walk in purpose.

Romans 8:28
And we know that in all things God works for the good of those who love him, who have been called according to his purpose.

_____

_____

_____

_____

_____

_____

_____

You Are Rooted In Purpose

You Are Rooted In Purpose

Now write down the direction you feel in your heart that God is leading you to walk into His purpose for your life.

_____

_____

_____

_____

_____

_____

_____

_____

_____

_____

_____

_____

You Are Rooted In Purpose

Day 16

Stay Positive

Whenever something unfavorable or challenging comes your way, **STAY POSITIVE**! It is so easy to become down, heavy laden or sad when something negative happens to you. In fact, most of us will simply begin to think about so many negative things and the consequences surrounding those things, that we produce a negative outcome in our lives. However, we should focus our thoughts on the positive things of God. We should focus on things that will produce solutions to what we are dealing with. It takes more effort to stay positive than it does to be negative. It is easy to want to give up and give in to a certain situation or thing we are dealing with. However, it takes a lot of effort to focus on something positive. But, you can do it. The next time you are faced with a troubling situation, take a moment, clear your mind and begin to focus on a positive solution to your problem. If something

Stay Positive

is bad, start thinking about something good. If something hurts, start thinking about something joyful. If something has been denied from you, start thinking about the things that God has prepared for you, that are on their way. Never stay negative in a negative situation. Become positive in a negative situation and watch positive things happen.

> **Never stay negative in a negative situation. Become positive in a negative situation and watch positive things happen.**

Write below how you will handle future disappointments and negative events you may encounter.

Philippians 4:8
Finally, brothers, whatever is true, whatever is noble, whatever is right, whatever is pure, whatever is lovely, whatever is admirable--if anything is excellent or praiseworthy--think about such things.

_____

_____

_____

Stay Positive

Stay Positive

Day 17

Get Your Expectations Up

Have you ever wondered why it seems like some people are getting blessed all the time? Have you ever wondered what it is that they are doing that you aren't? Have you ever wondered what is missing that is stopping you from receiving your blessings? Well, the answer lies in the fact that they simply have learned a great secret that you haven't. That secret is that they have simply gotten their expectations up. Yes! You must learn how to expect something if you hope to receive something. So, what are you hoping for? What do you desire? What are you anticipating to happen in your life that will change you positively? If you can't think of anything, then don't expect anything.

> **You must learn how to expect something if you hope to receive something**

Get Your Expectations Up

We simply have to get our expectations up. Dare to dream! Dare to hope! Dare to plan! Do all these things with an eager expectation that God has put these things in your heart and He will be faithful to watch them come to pass. Don't be afraid to seek God and ask Him to give you something to hope for. Don't be afraid to seek God and ask Him to give you a bigger home, car, better health, more money, a loving heart, or the ability to forgive, etc. Seek Him, find Him, ask Him, wait for Him and operate in Him. Go ahead and get your expectations up. Think bigger than any obstacle you may be facing! Think better than any negative comment you have ever heard someone say about you! Think further than any curve being thrown at you! Think deeper than any hurt you may have ever experienced! Focus your attention on the goodness of God and all that He has for you. All that He has for you is waiting on you! Write below and ask God to give you the ability to expect something great from Him. Next, ask God to help you focus your attention on the things He has for you and not on the things trying to keep you from receiving God's best in your life.

Get Your Expectations Up

Acts 3:5

So the man gave them his attention, expecting to get something from them.

Get Your Expectations Up

Day 18

Don't Sell Yourself Short

There are two things you should never forget in this lifetime. Never sell yourself short and never give up. We sell ourselves short when we don't strive to achieve higher things.

> **Never sell yourself short and never give up**

It is so easy to become comfortable in life and not want anything else. It is very easy to convince ourselves that we have accomplished everything that we set out to do and now it is time to sit back and take it easy. However, a lot of times when we do this, we are selling ourselves short. You can sell yourself short when you don't achieve everything that God planned for you to do. You can sell yourself short when you fool yourself into thinking that you did something worthwhile when it really wasn't worthwhile at all. The easiest way to make sure we don't sell ourselves short is to set goals and standards for ourselves often. We should always set out to do something or accomplish something that we have never done before. As a result, we will grow, evolve and live a more full and gratifying life. The next thing we must remember is to never quit. It is easy to quit when things get tough. It is easy to quit when we get tired of trying to accomplish something. However, we must be mindful that quitters never win and winners never quit. In order to push ourselves into a new level of achievement, we must learn how to press ourselves through our challenges.

Press through your challenge and get to your blessing

The next time you feel discouraged, press through it. The next time you want to quit, press through it. The next time you don't think something is worth your time and effort and you want to quit, press through it. When we can learn how to press towards our goals, we will be able to press through our pain and press towards our blessing. Press on! Press on to greatness! Press on to a better lifestyle! Press on to more money! Press on to better health! Press on to a better marriage! Press on to a better relationship with God! – Press On!

Write below how you will press on when being challenged while striving to achieve new things in your life.

Philippians 3:14 (NIV)
I press on toward the goal to win the prize for which God has called me heavenward in Christ Jesus.

_____

_____

_____

_____

_____

_____

_____

_____

_____

Day 19

Be Thankful

Giving thanks is the key to success in life. We can't thank God enough. We should never forget all the good things that He has done for us. If it was not for His goodness, we would not be able to do the things we do. We would not be able to eat, rest or have joy in our lives if it wasn't for His goodness. That's why we should thank Him all the time. You must begin to always set aside a certain part of your day and begin to just thank God. Thank Him for his mercy, because we definitely don't deserve His blessings. Thank Him for His kindness because we do so many things wrong each day and yet, He still loves us. Thank Him for His promises because if it wasn't for His promises, we would have no hope at all. And, if we have no hope, we have nothing to look forward to. We must thank Him for choosing to have a relationship with us and making Himself known to us. Without His presence in our lives,

Be Thankful

we would be lost and aimlessly walking around trying to figure out what we should do. We should thank Him for His protection. If we only knew how many times that He has sent Angels to block us from harm, hurt and destruction, we would get on our knees and cry out aloud our gratitude towards Him. Finally, we should continuously thank God for thinking enough of us to give us a guarantee of everlasting life by simply confessing with our mouths and believing in our hearts that Jesus Christ is our Lord and Savior.

As the old folks used to say, "If he never does anything else for me again, He has already done enough." Take some time now and write below a thank you note to God Almighty. Start out by saying, Lord, I just want to thank you for…

1 Chronicles 16:8

Give thanks to the Lord, call on his name; make known among the nations what he has done.

_____

_____

_____

Be Thankful

Be Thankful

Day 20

Know Where Your Help Comes From

Have you ever needed help and felt as if no one was there for you? Does it sometime feel like no one really cares for you? Have you ever thought that you would never be able to do something without help from someone else? If you have, you are not alone. Sometimes when you need help the most, there seems to be no one around at all. Well, guess what? There is always help for us when we are in need of it. However, we must look for our help in the right person. Our help always comes from the Lord. Yes! He is always there waiting on us to call on Him. So, the next time you are in need of help, call on Him immediately. Don't panic, just simply call on Him for help. Don't give up; call on Him when you need help. It is really easier than you think. Also, keep in mind that we shouldn't call on God only when we are in trouble or need something. That is the wrong approach to take in order to get Help from

Know Where Your Help Comes From

Him. Start calling on God for help before you do something. Call on Him for help before you buy something. Call on Him for help before you accept that job. Call on Him for help before you date someone. Call on Him for help in advance! Too many people call on God after they do something that is detrimental or wrong. They then call on Him for help because they want relief from their bad decisions, etc. However, we should call on Him for His help before we do anything.

Yes! Don't be too prideful to call on God for His help before you do anything. It is a great way to know that you will be walking in His will and His blessings. Write below things that you know you need to call on God and ask Him for help with right now.

Psalms 121:2

My help comes from the Lord, the Maker of heaven and earth.

_____

_____

_____

Know Where Your Help Comes From

Know Where Your Help Comes From

Day 21

Image Is Everything

Never forget that you have been created in the image of the greatest architect in the universe. You are a divine creation. You are like God in the sense that you are able to live a great life, rule over certain things and overcome many things. The life that God has given you is very precious and must be treated as such. We have been given the ability to make choices, name things and create things. The ability to choose and make decisions is what gives us our divinity. Yes! We have been given the ability to create the type of life we want to live. We should never forget that our choices create our realities.

> **Our choices create our realities.**

Adam and Eve were created with the opportunity to choose the reality that they wanted to live. They chose the wrong things and that led to a very difficult and painful reality for

Image Is Everything

them. You don't have to live in the painful realities of life that they did. You were created in His image. That means that when people see you, they should see Him. God isn't known for always being sad; we shouldn't be known that way either. People's image of God is one of power. Our image should be the same. When people think of God, they think of abundance, our life should reflect abundance as well. People view God as being very confident. Therefore, when they see us, they should see confidence coming from us as well. The question then is, are we giving a true reflection of who God is to others? Think about that and make a decision to create a new life for yourself. When others see us they should see God's nature and power in us. They should see joy in us! They should see peace in us! They should see *"the best"* in us! They should see all of God's qualities in us. You can create a new life and find your greatest self right now! You can discover your greatest self right now by choosing the path that has been laid out for you by God before you were ever born. The path to living a prosperous and fulfilling life is very simple and easy for you to choose. All you have to do is believe in God the Father, Christ Jesus and the Holy Spirit. Next,

Image Is Everything

you have to believe that God the Father who is Jehovah, is the Most High God. Next, you must believe that Jesus Christ is your Lord and Savior by confessing with your mouth and believing that with your heart. Finally, you must trust in the Holy Spirit to be your best friend whom will stick by you and counsel you daily. If you can do that, your path will be full of joy and success for the rest of your life starting right now. When you give your life to Jesus Christ, you become born again. To be born again, means you have found your greatest self. Now that you have found your greatest self, you must walk in your gifting. You can easily know that you have what it takes by doing the following: (1) Buy a Bible that you can understand. (2) Read it every day. (3) Pray to God daily, (4) Find a local church, join it and attend it regularly (5) Ask the Holy Spirit to reveal to you daily all about God the Father and the Son and finally, (6) help others choose the same path you have decided to choose, that is Christ Jesus. Every day as you walk closer in your relationship with God, you will discover all of who you are that you never knew. Get ready to possess new territories! Discover joy! Discover riches! Discover peace! Discover God and *"Discover Your*

Greatest Self!" Write below your new journey that you want to take as you begin to discover your greatest self, knowing that you have what it takes to be all that you were born to be!!

Genesis 1:26-27

Then God said, "Let us make man in our image, in our likeness, and let them rule over the fish of the sea and the birds of the air, over the livestock, over all the earth, and over all the creatures that move along the ground." ²⁷ So God created man in his own image, in the image of God he created him; male and female he created them.

_____

_____

_____

_____

_____

_____

Image Is Everything

Epilogue

One of the best ways to begin to discover your greatest self is for you to accept Christ Jesus as your Lord and Savior. If you have never done this, repeat these simple words and it will be a done deal. Repeat the following: Lord Christ Jesus as of this very moment, I accept you as Lord and Savior of my life. I now give my life to you to be fashioned for your purpose and glory. Lord, all of these things that I have said, I truly believe in my heart and have confessed with my mouth to you. I know now that I have received everlasting life based on the work that Christ has done and will continue to do in my life. Lord Christ, thank you for bringing me to this point of my life where I surrender my all to you. It is in the Holy Spirit through Christ Jesus, I say Amen.

Humbly Yours in Christ,

Apostle Jamie T. Pleasant

Epilogue

Books by Dr. Pleasant

Book Dr. Pleasant for a Speaking Engagement

For speaking engagements, please contact Dr. Jamie T. Pleasant at admin@newzionchristianchurch.org or 678.845.7055

All of Dr. Pleasant's books can be can be purchased at any bookstore or online at https://www.amazon.com/-/e/B0036Q4L6E ,barnesandnoble.com and others

Books by Dr. Pleasant

About the Author

About the Author

Dr. Jamie T. Pleasant; Ph.D. is a tenured marketing professor at Clark Atlanta University, which is an AACSB accredited institution of higher learning. This educational achievement of AACSB accreditation. is the highest and most distinguished accredited affiliation of business schools around the entire world. He is also the Chief Executive Pastor and Founder of New Zion Christian Church in Suwanee, Georgia. As a modern day polymath, he holds a bachelor's degree in Physics from Benedict College in Columbia, South Carolina, Marketing Studies from Clemson University and an M.B.A. in Marketing from Clark Atlanta University. On August 13, 1999, Apostle Pleasant achieved a Georgia Tech milestone by becoming the first African American to graduate with a Ph.D. in Business Management.

God gave him the vision to establish a Biblically based economic development initiative for New Zion Christian Church. He remains at the pulse of the economic business sector. As a result, Apostle Pleasant is in constant

About the Author

demand to train, speak and teach others at all levels in ministries and the private sector about business and economic development across the country. He has created cutting edge and industry leading ministerial programs in the church such as The Financial Literacy Academy For Youth (FLAFY), where youth from the ages of 13-19 attend 12 week intense classes on financial money management principles. At the end of 12 weeks, they receive a "Personal Finance" certificate of achievement. He also founded in 2016, The Young Leaders and Success Academy (YLASA), where students between the ages of 10-21 learn leadership, presentation, creative thinking and problem solving skills. At the end of three months, they receive certificates of achievements for various courses. Other ministries he has pioneered include; The Wealth Builders Investment Club (WBIC), which educates and allows members to actively invest in the stock market, along with the much celebrated Institute of Entrepreneurship Innovation and creativity (IOE), where participants earn a certificate in Entrepreneurship after three months of comprehensive training in all aspects of starting and owning a successful competitive business. The

About the Author

main goal and purpose of IOE is that each year one of the trained businesses will be awarded up to $10,000 startup money to ensure financial success. The newly added SAT & PSAT prep courses for children ages 9-19 fuels the potential success of all who walk through the doors of New Zion Christian Church.

Apostle Pleasant has met with political officials such as President Clinton and Nelson Mandela. He has delivered the opening prayer for the born again Christian and comedian, Steve Harvey. He has performed marriage ceremonies and counseled numerous celebrated personalities such as Usher Raymond (Confessions Recording Artist), Terri Vaughn (Lavita Jenkins on The Steve Harvey Show), and many others.

He is civically engaged as well. After the Columbine High School shooting, he founded the National School Safety Advocacy Association. His latest foundations include the Young Entrepreneurship Program (YEP) and the African American Consumer Economic Rights (AACER).

He has authored thirteen (13) books, *Prayers That Open Heaven, Capturing and Keeping the Pastor's Heart,*

About the Author

Powerful Prayers That Open Heaven, Advertising Principles: How to Effectively Reach African Americans in the 21st Century, Discover a New You, From My Heart To Yours: Love Letters From A Loving Father, Today's Apostle: Servants of God, Leading His People towards Unity , Strategic Health Marketing: Marketing Mix and Segmentation Strategies, Daily Quotes for Daily Blessings, The Importance of Subcultural Marketing, I'm Just Sayin...,The Making of A Man and You Have What It Takes: A 21 Day Discovery of Your Greatest Self.

Dr. Pleasant is the husband of Kimberly Pleasant (whom he loves dearly) and the proud father of three children: Christian, Zion and Nacara.

FINI

www.ingramcontent.com/pod-product-compliance
Lightning Source LLC
LaVergne TN
LVHW011424080426
835512LV00005B/257